Candi's Demise

BK PUBLISHING CO.

AKNOWLEDGEMENTS

First all praise due to the most high most merciful Allah(swt) for giving me the strength and endurance as well as blessings in this thing called life. I'm forever thankful to my mother Gale and sister Angelique for always having that bail money ready lol just kidding thanks for always holding me down no matter what. Watching you two has taught me that anything in life is possible and I can always turn a negative to a positive. Most importantly my daughter Maisa thank you for showing me what unconditional love is & giving me a reason to change, remain focused and level up. You're such an intelligent, sweet, and loving daughter. Next, I would like to personally (very personally lol) thank my soulmate Tameka. I appreciate and love you so much Thank you for showing me what real love and a healthy relationship is. I'm so grateful that you, Envy and Ahmaad are in my life. Of course, this book wouldn't have been possible without my dope ass friends Zairaih, Monique, Brittany, Quasimah and Andrea for always inspiring me by motivating me to be the best. From Day one, my homie Captain told me I had a story to tell and that I should write a book. "Well, here it is Big Homie" thanks for all the support and encouragement! Also Bintu, owner and publisher of BK Publishing giiiiiirl your amazing, thank you! I also cannot forget my favorite therapist who was also my Doula and the one who held my hand as I delivered my child. Saleemah, if only you knew how many times you kept me grounded! Thank you for everything. Now y'all know I had to save THE BEST for last ... (drumroll please)...MYSELF lol Leo shit haha. I thank myself for overcoming so many obstacles meant to destroy me and remaining my authentic self in the process. This one's for me and anyone who is faced with adversity and feels like giving up…Don't!!

TABLE OF CONTENTS

Ch. 1- Judgement Day……....Pg. 5

Ch. 2- Distant Strangers……Pg. 12

Ch. 3- The Beginning……...Pg. 20

Ch. 4- Revenge……………...Pg. 29

Ch. 5- Locked Down……......Pg. 37

Ch. 6- Candi's Regret….…...Pg. 50

Ch. 7- Playing With Fire…...Pg. 59

Ch. 8- Dead or Alive……….Pg. 67

Ch. 9- Love & Marriage……Pg. 74

Ch. 10- Playing With Fire….Pg. 83

Chapter 1
Judgement Day

"Ms. Gordon, do you have any last words to say before your sentencing today?"

My lawyer looked at me hesitantly and mouthed the word "no" but I knew my rights and I wasn't gonna back down not now or ever. This was my time to shine. I stood up proudly with my chest in the air and my Philly attitude and said, "Yes your honor, I do."

Reaching into my pocket, I located the piece of paper that was folded up perfectly into a square and started reading from the top. "Your Honor I stand before you today with no regrets of what I did that day. "I stopped and took a deep Breath.

"I had no options; I couldn't walk away! So yes! I did what I did. Now give me my time so I can do my bid. Matter of fact give me a mink I'll do it on my back. Or some true religion jeans and I'll do it on my knees. Maybe even some stilettos so I can do it on my toes." The blood was pumping now as I stood defiant.

"It was my life or hers and I wasn't ready to go. So judge, go ahead. Do whatever it is you gone do I make anything look good orange or blue."

When I got done I could hear the gasps and whispers in the courtroom. My lawyer's face was red, the judge had a blank stare, and my sister burst out into tears. Truth was, I was way too ignorant and young to understand the consequences of my actions at that time. I would soon learn that it pays the cost to be the boss.

"Thank you, Ms. Gordon, you may be seated. It has been made clear to me and the Municipal courts of Pennsylvania that you absolutely show no remorse for the devastation that you have caused Ms. Robinson."

A chill went through my spine.

"Not only have you committed bodily harm to another human being that has ended in reconstructive surgery and therapy, but the psychological damage to the plaintiff is done. This will impact her for years to come. Young people today need to keep their emotions in check because no wrongdoing will go unpunished. Hard lessons have to be learned each and every day, you're lucky she didn't die. Then we would be talking a different story and we would be discussing Murder instead of attempted murder. With that said, I sentence you to 5-10 years in a state correctional facility. You have the right to appeal......."

I zoned the fuck out and didn't even hear the rest of what she was saying. Suddenly the weight of my current reality hit me like a ton of bricks. Did she just say I would do ten years in prison? I started sobbing loudly and yelled at my lawyer. "TEN YEARS? DID SHE JUST SAY TEN?!"

My lawyer hugged me tight and whispered in my ear "Calm down, calm down. You may get out early for good behavior and only end up doing five." There was hope for me after all.

The bailiff walked up to me and out came two prison guards ready to take me away. I turned to my family and mouthed "I love you." Before letting them handcuff me, I took off my diamond earrings that my mother had given me and gave them to my sister.

"Take care of them for me. I'll be back."
And turned to be taken away.

How did a girl like me end up doing prison time?

Chapter 2
Distant Strangers

"Mommy, mommy look"

Myelah, my six-year-old daughter was pointing at a kid in the park who had just fell off the slide and was crying loudly. I walked up to the little boy who looked about the same age to see if he needed help.

As I approached closer, a woman appeared and instantly bent down.

"What's wrong Khalil are you ok?" The kid, after seeing that his knee was bleeding a little cried louder." Suddenly I remembered I had a few band aids in my pocketbook and a lollipop. As a mom you never knew when you would need either. I decided to gently interject.

"Hi! I'm Aleisia, my daughter was playing by the swings and saw him fall so we came over here to see if we can help. I have this tissue, a band aid and lollipop if you would like to have it."

"Sure! Thank you we really appreciate it" The woman looked up to grab the items from my hands but she looked like she had seen a ghost.

Time felt like it had stopped for a million seconds. Turns out we had both just seen a ghost and one recognized the other.

In another life she was my woman, my codefendant, and my partner in crime. But today, she looked completely different.... she was basically a stranger.

Her locs which used to adorn every inch of her head, were now shaved off into a fade and cut low and she had put on a significant amount of weight. But her eyes...... you never ever forget those piercing eyes and her full lips that I used to love kissing. She once knew her way over every inch of my body causing me to do things you only read about in erotic stories. Back then she could make me quiver with just a touch of her hands gently squeezing my breasts to place into her mouth and even in this moment her gaze felt very familiar.

"Candi?" She recognized me too and we both locked our eyes into each other.

"Mommy, whose that!" The sound of Myelah's little voice broke the silence.

"Oh honey, this is mommy's friend Ms. Ty. Mommy hasn't seen her in a long time."

Tykisha or "Ty" as the streets affectionately called her because she felt her real name was too girly, turned her attention to my daughter and said, "Hey Lil mama. I'm Ms. Ty, and this is my nephew Scooter."

Myelah smiled at her and said, "Hi Ms. Ty. Hi Scooter. Want to play on the seesaw with me Scooter?" Scooter, now smiling from the lollipop I had given Ty looked up for permission.

"Go ahead young Bull. Just let me put this bandaid on you first." Then we watched the children run off to play.

****

"How have you been" Ty asked me.

"Good" I replied.

"I can see that. You look good and happy."

"I am" I said.

"Man it's been a minute."

This time I didn't respond. I let the silence linger.

"Why did you stop picking up my calls after I got out?"

This was it. This was the moment I had been waiting for. My moment of truth.

"Because I didn't think there was anything left to talk about."

Ty had gotten out two years before me and by the time I got out, we were broken up. I wanted to leave the past behind me. She was a major part of the reason we had both been incarcerated and it brought back so many memories.

In order for me to move forward, I had to start from the beginning .....

Chapter 3
The Beginning

"Baby I'm about to leave. I gotta meet this fein." Ty woke me up with a light kiss on my forehead. This was her usual morning routine. She always got up at the crack of dawn and left out before me. Since I didn't have to be at work until 9am, I checked my phone and saw that it was only 6am closed my eyes, rolled back over onto my stomach, and said, "Ok have a good day and don't forget to take the trash out. Love you." Ty opened the cabinet to where her stash was hidden and grabbed a bag full of crack vials then locked up the remainder and took the trash from out of the kitchen closing the door behind her.

I laid my head all the way onto the pillow and sighed. I really hated that she sold drugs. When we met, I was 14 and living with my mother who was addicted to crack cocaine. She knew about all of this because I told her. It bonded us even deeper because her mother was also an addict. It was only after a year of us being together that I found out Ty was her own mothers supply and one of the biggest drug dealers in Germantown. But, by then I was in too deep to leave. She spoiled me with the finer things in life and introduced me to all the luxury brands Christian Dior, Gucci, Louis Vuitton, so I fell hard and fast.

Ty was the type of person who took care of everybody. From her little brother to her grandmother, her mom, and especially me. She never really got to experience a normal childhood which made me feel sad for her. By the time we met she was already a high school dropout and was selling drugs to support her entire family. Although my mother was using, she always said to me "I don't care what you do. Just take your ass to school." So that's exactly what I did.

But, laying there this morning I still wondered how the hell I ended up with a drug dealer when I hated them because of all the chaos and destruction they caused in black families. Drugs left us feeling broken, so I guess it was that same brokenness that attracted us to one another. When we met it was just as friends. I was dating her friend Stacy but she wasn't honest and was lying about her age so I ended up breaking up with her later moving onto Ty. Things were complicated at first but we couldn't stay away from each other. A couple of years later we moved in together and started a life.

Living with Ty had some good days but was toxic as shit. While I went to school and worked as an administrative assistant, she ran the streets. She was always getting caught cheating with other bitches and our arguments would sometimes end up in physical altercations. Our relationship was very rocky and filled with drama. We fought just as hard as we loved. Sometimes I felt like we were fighting to stay together when we should have just stayed apart.

The alarm went off at 7:30am and I got out of bed and made myself a cup of coffee. Dark with a little bit of hazelnut cream and sugar, just the way I liked it. I ran the shower in the bathroom and put on some old school Anita baker to get ready for my day. After I got out I slipped on some khaki chinos, a white button up, and my favorite brown Gucci loafers. I remembered that I had some leftover Buffalo chicken dip in the fridge from the night before that I could pack that for my lunch. I grabbed my lunch box and filled it up with food. Then I grabbed my car keys and walked out the front door.

When I got to my car, I immediately stopped in my tracks. "WHAT THE FUCK!" I yelled out loud. My motherfucking windshield wipers were broken off and a note was slid in the front window. "You a corny bitch that need to leave Ty alone." It read. I didn't even have to see a name to know who would do something like this.

Ashley. That bitch was Ty's ex or rather her old side piece. She never could get over the fact that she moved on I don't know if she missed the free weed or sex, but it was over and she needed to get that into her brain. I was pissed off but decided to stay calm until I saw Ty after work. My money came first before anything.

When I got home that night I burst into the apartment with the note in my hand yelling Ty's name over and over again "Ty, Ty, TY!!!" She came out of the kitchen looking scared "What? What's going on baby!"
"Why the fuck is this Bitch harassing me? Is you fucking her still or something because this shit just got weird. She broke my windshield wipers and left this note." I threw the paper across the table to Ty and she was too quiet for my liking. "Why are you so silent? Are you fucking her or not?!" Ty

dropped her head down and started crying, "I fucked up. I went to serve her last week when she called and said she wanted some bud but then we fucked. It was only one time baby you gotta believe me!" I snapped and slapped the shit out of her face. My anger flared up and I kept punching wherever I could not knowing where my punches would land.

Once I calmed down, I said "This bitch is YOUR PROBLEM. Deal with it or I'm gon have to deal with her." Instead of leaving Ty, from that moment on I knew I would get back any way that I could. Nobody makes a fool out of Candi.

CHAPTER 4
Revenge

It was ladies night at Temptations night club and I was headed out tonight. Ty was staying at her grandmother's house because she wasn't feeling too good. I told her not to worry about rushing home to me and to do what she needed to do. I did my make up and put on this sexy black sheer camisole dress and sprayed on my YSL perfume she had bought me for my birthday two months ago. I finished the look with Christian Louboutin pumps and a matching clutch. A bitch was looking like a bag of money.

You could see the outline of my breasts and hips under the moonlight as I switched my way over to the car. I hadn't been out in awhile and was feeling myself. I popped in my R-Kelly cd and grooved to "Jeep" as I sped down I-76 to Delaware Ave where the club was located.

When I got to the club, the line was all the way down the street. I valeted my car and walked right to the front. "Candi?" I looked up and saw where the voice was coming from: "Oh what's up Jason! I didn't know you worked here." Jason used to date my sister when I was younger and grew up with us around the way. "Oh yea I started a couple of months ago. You by yourself?" I shook my head yes. "Aight bet Imma let you in this motherfucker. Don't worry bout nuffin."

I was lucky as shit. Not only was I getting in for free but because I knew him, but they weren't checking my ID which was a good thing because I didn't have one since I was only 19. I could already tell that tonight was gonna be a good night. As I walked by him he said, "Tell ya sis I said what up too!" I smiled and nodded my head in his direction. But really, my sister had a whole new man and wasn't thinking bout him.

You could hear the bitches sucking their teeth and talking shit as I was lead in the door. *Yea I am that bitch,* I thought to myself. When I got in, the club was turned up. Smoke was creeping onto the dance floor and strobe lights were flashing all around the room. I made my way past a group of women and walked straight to the bar. It was time to get drunk. "What you need sweetie?" The bartender asked me. "Ciroc and cranberry" I yelled over the hip hop music. "Ten" she yelled back and I gave her a 20 dollar bill. When the bartender came back with my drink and change, I left her the other $10 as a tip. Ty taught me how to take care of people. She smiled at me, and I winked at her. I was really feeling myself tonight.

I was vibing to the music and dancing by myself when she caught my eye. She was dancing across from me surrounded by friends. I knew it was her because of her long and pretty ass hair that she wore in box braids. She had on fresh Gibaud jeans and a white t-shirt. I walked over and started dancing with her and she ran her hands all over my hips. I turned around and when she saw it was me she was dancing with, rubbed on my ass harder. "Crystal, Crystal, Crystal" I whispered in her ear.

We both knew that what we were doing was forbidden because Ashley would kill us both. But I didn't care. I wanted to fuck her bitch like she fucked mine.

I bought us some shots and by the time we were on our third I was letting her finger me in the club and she was begging me to fuck her. I took her home that night with me no questions asked. As soon as we got in the door she stripped naked and I started eating her pussy from the back while she bent over my couch. I spread her ass cheeks apart and fucked her asshole with my tongue and squeezed her breasts at the same time. She went crazy. After she came, we went to the bedroom and she laid me down and placed her face in between my legs sucking and tugging on my clit gently.

I reached for my side drawer and pulled out my dildo and prepared to turn her out. She seemed nervous at first because she usually did the fucking but she was willing to let me take charge. She ate my pussy next with my vibrator and her wet tongue and I cried out "CRYSTAL" as I came hard, long, and fast. We fucked all night and she called a cab before the sun came up.

After she left I played with my pussy again. The sex was so good and I was still turned up. Damn I want some more. I thought to myself. I wouldn't mind fucking her again. I think I should have it all.

So I did. Over the next few months I kept fucking Ashley's girlfriend every chance I got. Then I got sloppy with it.

CHAPTER 5
Locked Down

Beep. Beep. Beep. The sound of the blaring alarm travelled through the cell block and you could hear all the inmates waking up to get ready for their day. Although I wasn't where I wanted to be, I was thankful that I got to share a cell with Ty in the county. After sentencing Ty and I were sent to the county and had been here almost two weeks. The only thing is we were separated from the general population in what they called "administrative segregation" and we were there with other women in the hole, spent an hour out a day, and fed through a slot. That shit was pathetic, but we were still here like Bonnie and Clyde. Administrative segregation is where we waited for the sheriff to pick us up and take us to a state correctional facility.

"Good morning baby," I said to Ty from up top my bunk bed. "Good morning. It would be a better morning if I could get the fuck outta here. Man this shit crazy" she responded back to me. I hated that she had to endure this with me. Deep down I blamed myself and felt guilty because she was locked up because of me. "I want to go home" she said real low to herself.

Clink. Clink. Clink. The sound of the keys opening the cell startled me. Gordon, Robinson, grab whatever you need. You're on your way outta here! My heart was beating fast as shit. "Where are we going?!" I asked the guard. "MUNCY state correctional facility."

****

As soon as we arrived at MUNCY I knew that everything would be different. Some good and some bad. Since Ty was tried as an adult in court, she was immediately placed in intake but because I was under the age of 22, I was placed in the Young Adult Offender Program. That was really the beginning of the end for us. Over the next few months we could only see each other during religious services and sneak kites as our method of communication. Kites were the letters we would write and fold up to fly over to someone discreetly. I would write letters professing my love to her and promising her the world when we got out. I felt so sorry and indebted to her that I never got to experience the shame of what I did to someone else.

After about six months of being at MUNCY, the day came when Ty had to be transferred to another facility, Cambridge Springs. One cold ass November morning I watched her leave in handcuffs and placed once again in the back of a prison van. I was devastated and now I felt really alone. We would still find a way to communicate via three-way mail through her grandmother who loved me. But, it would be years before I would physically see her face again.

*****

At MUNCY I was like a kid in a Candy Store. There were bitches everywhere.

Short bitches, tall bitches, Puerto Rican bitches, bitches with phat asses, some of the baddest. And I wanted to sample it all. But little did I know that I was the actual prey and the other inmates were the hunters. "Wassup fresh meat." The girls in the kitchen would say to me every morning. Kitchen duty was a part of my prison responsibilities. I got a job working the breakfast and lunch shift which gave me a chance to have access to all the baddies. Sometimes an inmate would stick their tongue out at me or blow me a kiss.

After a while I took the bait and started fucking with some of the women on the side. Ty was out of sight out of mind, and I was young and horny. Out of all the bitches in there, Keisha was my favorite. She was born and raised in Brownsville, NYC, tall with curvy hips and beautiful with long dreadlocks that I loved to run my fingers through. She also had a nice ass and body with hips and ass that you could see through her jail jumpsuit. All the inmates loved to talk about how thick she was. Plus, she was smart as shit because we would always have intellectual conversations about the future. She and Ty were like night and day. Keisha was down to earth and someone who had dreams and ambitions. She was in prison because of a crime she committed out of love for her family. Ty was someone who loved money and was headed back to the streets regardless because all she knew and wanted to know was the drug game. It was refreshing meeting someone who wanted more for themselves but sad to know she would always remain behind bars because of her sentencing.

It seemed like everything about Keisha was perfect. But there was only one problem…. she was serving 30-70 years for murdering her little sister's rapist. Everybody on the inside would say "Don't get in no relationship with no lifer because they will keep you there." I didn't want to listen though. I still fell for her. As the days grew longer, spending time with her made them feel a lot shorter. We would eat together, shower together, do whatever. She was my main chick and she knew that. "You the finest thing in here" I would tell her while smacking her ass and pulling her locs.

*****

"Gordon! You've got mail!" The inmate on mail duty handed me a letter before leaving the room. I hadn't written to her in MONTHS. Shit I had almost forgot about her but I damn sure ripped the letter open as soon as I saw Ty's name. *Dear Candi, wassup with you shortie. I hope you still doing good. I know you're still looking good. I ain't want much I just didn't want you to be the last to know but I'm not doing too good. I been really sick the last two months. They said it's probably Anemia but it feels like I'm dying. If I am, the one wish I have is to see that pretty face again…. ."* Tears started dropping from my eyes and at that moment I decided that I was gonna get transferred from MUNCY to Cambridge Springs to see her.

My loyalty was too great and she had sacrificed so much for me. But Keisha couldn't know shit or she would try and fight me to stay longer. I couldn't compromise that.

There was only one way to get to Ty. I was already enrolled In the cosmetology program at MUNCY and decided to put in a transfer to attend the cosmetology program at Ty's prison. I figured that not only would I be closer to her but I would also have access to more resources because they had a better program. As much as I had made up my mind, I didn't have the guts to tell Keisha. Over the next few weeks as I waited for the decision to be made, I carried on normally and did everything like nothing was changing between us. I felt bad inside but what the fuck could I do about it? I would have to take this one to the grave because my loyalty to Ty depended on it.

****

Keisha and I were sitting out on the yard playing cards when the superintendent walked up to us. "Ms. Gordon, I have good news for you. You're headed to Cambridge Springs." I had this pretend look of shock on my face, "What?!" The Superintendent responded "Oh you didn't know? Well you're out of here shortly. You've been accepted into their cosmetology program." Then she walked off leaving me there with my palms sweating. Keisha was the first to say something to me. "Why didn't you tell them you didn't want to go?" "What can I do? If they say I gotta leave than I gotta leave. I'm so fucking mad I'm leaving you boo!!!" I was going straight to hell for all that lying I was doing. Didn't matter though. The next day, we said our goodbyes and I was out of there.

I was so nervous to see her again because we were now two completely different people.

CHAPTER 6
Candi's Regret

It was late when we arrived at Cambridge Springs. The inmates were all having dinner. As soon as we dropped off our stuff in our cells and went to eat our meal, I spotted Ty sitting in the crowd with a few people. She looked up and spotted me too. Her eyes got really wide. She didn't expect me to be there. I didn't expect her to look so bad. She was nothing but skin and bones! Definitely not the woman I used to curl up to in bed at night. You could tell the sickness had taken over her body and she had this look of defeat in her eyes. But she smiled as soon as she saw me and you could see it brought life right back into her. "Damn baby! Jail made that body look good! I ain't even know you was gon be here! I'm hype as shit right now! I got my baby back with me." She gave me a big ass hug and took me over to the food station. We sat together in silence as I ate my first few bites. I thought I would be happier to be there but I was actually really uncomfortable. I haven't seen this girl for so damn long. Like what the fuck was I really doing here?

As I was eating I saw someone staring at me from across the room. "You know that bitch or something?" She turned around and looked. "Oh Nae Nae? She just cool peeps." In the pit of my stomach I knew better. "Well she doesn't seem too cool. If she keep lookin at me like that I'm gon slap the shit outta her." She broke out in laughter. "Same ole' Candi, talking that tough shit."

"But you know I back it up to" I said. "Calm down. This the reason we in here now. But i want you to meet my home girl Moe." She turned her body to scan the room and yelled out to the dark-skinned girl across the room eating with her mouth open wide. The girl nodded her head what's up and got up to walk towards us. "What's up!" she greeted me with a big smile. "Whose this cutie pie?" "Oh this my boo Candi she just got down here from MUNCY. I ain't seen her in a minute but she's here to stay." Moe gave her a confused look that I would later find out was because Ty wasn't exactly being the most honest at the time. But she shook it off and said to me "Nice to meet you Candi hopefully we get acquainted and I can show you the ropes around here." Then she walked off.

Being at Cambridge Springs was like starting over again but presented an entirely new challenge. Although I liked

Cambridge because they had way more opportunities for inmates to get their certifications, it was the type of place where everybody knew everything. As soon as I arrived I was a target because I represented the unknown and people wanted to figure me out. Shit, I wanted to figure some of them out too. That's why I had to stay low about the women I would talk to but each time I met a girl I liked, here go Ty acting out tryna ruin it. But that shit ain't stop me from doing my own thing. I quickly learned that Ty wasn't exactly just waiting around for my love either.

One day while walking in the yard I saw Nae Nae and Ty talking in a low whisper but they ain't see me. I quietly walked in the opposite direction and went straight up to Moe who was busy talking with a group of girls. "Ayo Moe let me holler at you for a minute." She got up and took a walk with me. "Who is that Bitch Nae Nae to Ty? She tryna down play shortie but I think they fucking."

Another inmate who was ear hustling blurted out, "Man, that's her bitch for real until yo ass came along!" Apparently Ty and Nae Nae were together before I came but as soon as Ty laid eyes on me again it was a wrap. It didn't really matter to me, I just hated people lying and playing in my face. So much time had passed and I wasn't as attracted to her after spending so much time apart but we still had history so she could have told me. I decided that day we were gonna break up.

During this time, I also had a fetish for turning butches into my bitches. Strapping up and fucking them gave me instant power even when they claimed they didn't take dick. In prison we made our own dildos called ole boys. Some were made out of toothbrushes with pads wrapped around them, ace bandages, or condoms and gloves from the commissary. I didn't know how to make a good one so one day I went to Moe and asked her to make me one. Moe was the top dawg when it came to making prison strap-ons. She knew how to make it nice and secure so I could have these bitches really on my dick. "Moe, what's up I need a strap."

Moe was cool with both me and Ty and we had gotten closer than we first were so I knew I was putting her in a tight spot. "Bitch what? You tryna get me fucked up?" She said to me in her squeaky voice. " Bitch we not even together no more, I told you that. This aint none of her business. Who gon tell her?" After a little convincing she made me one and I went to pursue the object of my desire. There was this bad bitch I wanted to fuck. Her name was Butta because her skin was smooth like butter and I needed that.

CHAPTER 7
Playing With Fire

Fucking Tys bestfriends' girl was the biggest mistake I could have made. It started a chain of events that ultimately ended me in prison when I should have been enjoying my young life. Ty would be on the streets, and I would have Crystal in our sheets. I knew Ty would never catch us because she had too many street responsibilities to tend to which is why she barely noticed anything was wrong. All she and I ever did was eat, sleep, take trips, shop, and fuck. I knew that her money came before anything.

Ashley on the other hand suspected something was going on but she didn't know who her girl was fucking with. One day she called Crystal's phone while we were fucking. "Hello, where the fuck you at?" You could hear her angrily through the phone. I didn't even let Crystal speak. Instead, I placed my fingers in her mouth and let her suck them while she moaned loudly, and I stroked her slowly. I asked her "Whose pussy is this?" And Ashley heard all of this. After recognizing my voice, Ashley was on a mission to expose my cheating. She would see Ty on the block and accuse me of fucking her girlfriend, but

Ty told her "Stop making up lies. Damn you still mad I left you for her?"

Ty came home but instead of being upset with me about a rumor, she said, "You know this Bitch Ashley came by hating on you tryna say you fucking Crystal. I told that Bitch to think again. She got us fucked up." I was so fortunate to have a woman that trusted me so I took it for granted and didn't stop cheating. It was too fun and I wanted both worlds. But as I continued having my cake and eating it too, the harassment intensified. It went from windshield wipers being broken to all four of my car tires being slashed on my brand-new Infiniti, breaking windows of my house with bricks, and she would call my job daily trying to get me fired. One day I caught her playing on my phone and I told her "For every tire that you slashed, I'm going to slash you. If I ever catch up to you, I'm gon kill you." And I believed every word of what I had said.

I was so caught up in what I wanted that I didn't stop to think about what Crystal wanted because she was just a pawn in my game. She was starting to get really attached. "Candi, I want to ask you something." She said one day while we were laid up after fucking.

"Wassup?" "You ever think about us leaving both and being together? I like what we have going on and I don't want it to end." I got the fuck up instantly because I already knew where this was going. "That's not a good idea! If you leave your girlfriend I'll never fuck you again in life!" I knew it was harsh but she got the message even though she still kept asking me over and over again.

Days went by I finally got my chance. Ashley was feeling herself and went up to Ty asking "How your girlfriend tires doing?" Meanwhile I was in the house cooking breakfast and talking to my homegirl Kelly about all the recent drama. Ty called on the other line to let me know Ashley had just arrived on the block talking shit. I told her "Come get me!" And clicked back over to tell Kelly "Ooh pick me up bitch!" I thought about it briefly but then said "Nah, we can't you on the other side of broad street. I'm gon come over when I'm done beating her ass."

When Ty pulled up to the house, she had another chick sitting in the back seat. I was pissed off. "What the fuck she doing here?" The girl spoke up and interjected "Chill Shorty I'm here to fuck her up for you so you don't get your hands dirty." That annoyed me even more. "I appreciate that and all sis but I gotta do this one myself you feel me?" She understood and we dropped her off along the way to the block. When I got to the block I pulled out the pocket knife I had hidden in my hoodie and walked right up to her.

The next thing I know I must have blacked out because the knife was wedged at the top of her forehead into her skull and blood was everywhere. Ty must have pushed me in the car because the next thing I remember was her driving us fast as shit to the house, taking off all my clothes, and pushing me into the shower.

I think I just killed somebody.

CHAPTER 8
Dead or Alive

I'm a murderer. I can't believe I just killed somebody. As I sat in the shower and let the water fall onto me, I kept seeing images of the knife stabbing her several times and the people on the block yelling "Yo she shot out!" I knew what I had just done was really bad but I also knew in the hood snitches get stitches and wasn't nobody gonna cooperate.

Ty stayed with me that night and was more concerned than I was. As soon as I put on some dry clothes and got in the bed, my phone rang. It was my girlfriend Kelly calling to tell me to turn on the news. Ty turned on the tv to the news and immediately I heard the reporter say, "Authorities are looking for any information on a stabbing of another young lady that occurred this morning on Chew and Chelten Ave. The victim is on life support at Einstein Hospital. There are no suspects at this time. If you or someone you know has any leading information that could help us make an arrest, please call 1800-655-4023."

I said into the phone, "Bitch why are you calling me if they said no suspects at the time! I gotta go to bed." And I hung up on Kelly.

"Oh shit." I said "I thought she died." I said to Ty.

"So what you gon do?" Ty asked me

"I ain't gon do shit. I'm gon do me and move like I been doing. She could still die for all I care." And that's what I did for the first few days after I stabbed Ashley. I continued going to work like nothing happened and we kept our ears to the streets. After about a week we found out that Ashley had gotten surgery because the knife was wedged into her forehead but right now she was still in recovery after her surgery and in a coma. The cops were at the hospital each day waiting for her to wake up and regain her strength so she could tell them what she knew. I silently prayed she died so that she couldn't testify and say anything. Never did I consider that I would actually have to go to jail. I felt invincible.

****

Ring. Ring. Ring. "Hello", I said sleepily through the phone. "Ashley woke up. She's not dead." Damn shit was getting hot. Suddenly the stakes were high and my one prayer was that she better not say shit to the cops. For the first few days that she was awake Ashley wasn't cooperating with the cops. But as she laid in the hospital and realized Ty didn't give a damn about her and that I was getting all the protection and support…. she decided to tell the cops about everything.

A warrant was put out for my arrest, and I knew I had to turn myself in. But to my surprise, Ty also got a warrant because she was my getaway driver and accomplice. The night before I turned myself in, I cried so bad because there was no other option. I called my mom and sister and told them everything that was going on and they cried with me.

The courts said I was a danger to the public so they denied me bond when I went in. I had to sit for three months until my trial. You would think I would have thought about my actions during that time, but I just waited for the shit to play out because she got what was coming to her and I wasn't about to fold now.

Maybe if Ty hadn't called me up that day or if she had shown her some concern while laying in the hospital or maybe if I had let the other chick in the car do my dirty work things would have turned out differently. But as I stood before the judge at my sentencing, I knew I had made my bed and I was going to lie in it. But I still didn't give a fuck.

CHAPTER 9
Love & Marriage

So much about my life had changed since Ty got out. I had successfully received my cosmetology license in prison and taken my state boards so I now worked in a salon and had gotten married………..to a man.

****

I met Yassir one day while walking downtown to the Gallery. Him and his cousin were shopping for a chain on jewelers' row and was about to grab some food in the food court. Everyone went shopping downtown and you never knew who you would run into. "Ayo shorty what's up with you? You are beautiful! Tell me you don't gotta man." I rolled my eyes and told him, "I don't, I actually got a girl." He didn't seem phased by that piece of information. "Oh yeah? That's what's up, but you can still make a new friend. You're too gorgeous to pass me by." And he was too cute and charming for me to deny. I gave him my number, a decision I would later come to regret.

At the time I was dating a chick from North Philly named Blizz. We had just started fucking and I liked her, but we didn't have much time in and I was still talking to some old flames. I started innocently talking to Yassir because I hadn't been with a man ever in my life so I didn't take it seriously at first. Yassir was Muslim and loved his religion, so much so that he refused to have sex with me because he was waiting until marriage. He prayed five times a day and spoke about Allah to me often. I was also Islamic by faith, but it had been years since I faithfully practiced and given my lifestyle I also shied away from the Muslim community in Philly. The more we talked, the greater the urge I had to make more changes in my life and strengthen my spirituality. He was so different from anyone else I had ever known. The icing on the cake was that we discovered he knew my brother from being incarcerated in his youth. He was building my trust and I needed someone I could respect and believe in. He became that and more.

****

Ring. Ring. Ring. "Hello, yes this is she." I said into the telephone. It was my doctor calling from her office telling me I had contracted an STD called Trichomoniasis. After she told me where to pick up my prescription. I hung the phone up fuming. "WHAT THE FUCK!" There was only one person who could have given it to me……….. Blizz. I called her up and cursed her the fuck out. "BITCH! YOU BURNT ME!" Blizz was pleading on the phone saying she was sorry and crying. But I hung up and changed my number. It was on that very day I decided to put my lesbian life behind me, submit to Allah's will, and be with Yassir.

Yassir was excited to have me. At first he treated me like a princess and we dated for three years before getting married. It seemed like as soon as I let him put the ring on my finger, things started to change. It wasn't a rapid change, it was gradual. It started with my style of clothing. I went from wearing the latest designer and trends to being fully garbed up and wearing my Kimar every single day. Whenever I would run into someone from the lesbian community, they would be shocked to see my transformation. But, I wanted to commit myself to the process because Yassir made me believe we could have the world. I had more faith in him than in Allah at times. It was scary. But he loved me, bought me flowers, and took care of his family.

Yassir didn't really allow or encourage communication with any friend from my past who was a lesbian. He was very insecure about it and wanted to erase the stigma of my gayness. He often questioned whether or not he was satisfying me in the bedroom, and I would reassure him but deep down he wasn't and we both knew the elephant in the room was that I would always be gay. I loved women.

After we got married, he asked me for a baby. I had been through so much and felt like I had experienced so many things already, I thought I was ready to settle down and be a mom. So, I said yes, and we had a daughter. For a short while he became once again the man I had fallen for. I guess becoming a father made him feel good about himself and he wanted to provide as much as possible for his family. He would argue with me about still wanting to work but I had always made my own money and still wanted to. It was the Leo in me. The greater my desire for independence, the stronger his grasp on my life. Things were starting to crumble in our household, and I started to live a daily hell.

He was a manipulator to the highest power and began what he called "punishing" me by treating me like a child every time I didn't do what he wanted. He said his wife was to "obey" him. On the days he wanted me in the house, he would lock me inside with two by four wood. I accepted all the mental, physical, and verbal abuse for a long time before I decided things needed to change. It took him doing the unthinkable for me to finally wake up and realize he didn't really love me.

CHAPTER 10
Playing With Fire

Playing with fire once again. That's how I got here in the first place. Yassir and I were living a toxic marriage and I decided that I would have an affair. I knew it could be a dangerous move but I didn't care. I needed someone to talk to and I felt so alone because nobody in my life knew about the abuse. I met Shonnie at the shop when she was delivering mail and we were just cool at first. She would stop by every day, and we would share a joke or she would just be really sweet to me and I needed that. Next thing you know we were exchanging numbers and doing lunch dates because I had to go home at night.

What we were doing was risky. One day Yassir decided to stop by and surprise me with some food for lunch and I wasn't there. I was with Shonnie in a hotel fucking on my lunchbreak. He blew up my phone and demanded I tell him where I was. I told him I had run out of product and was on my way back from the hair store. This calmed him down, but it also put him on alert. Suddenly he watched my movements extra hard and turned up the surveillance. Shonnie would text me randomly and call but he didn't know of anybody named Shonnie from my past or in my family, so he started to catch on that something was off. He would pick arguments with me first thing in the morning and started asking to see my phone. I never kept anything incriminating in my phone from her so it drove him crazy not knowing what was going on.

This went on for a few months before he caught on to my lies. One of Yassir's cousins knew Shonnie and had seen us together one day while out eating. They told him and I had to confess that I had met somebody else. "YOU A FUCKING WHORE! SO YOU GON FUCK UP

YOUR FAMILY FOR SOME PUSSY?!"
The next thing I knew, I was laid out in the hospital with tubes coming out of me on life support………..

GLOSSARY

In this novel the main character, Candi, lived a life that many can relate to, or know of someone else who has experienced similar things. A lot of times in life we are involved in some type of dysfunctional relationship or another. Whether it be a friendship, familial, or intimate relationship. We all have those moments where we think "I should have saw the signs." I know I have....

Here's a checklist I created for those who may be confused, questioning if the relationship is safe, or feel like they need to leave:

Codependency

- Difficulty making decisions in a relationship
- Difficulty identifying your feelings
- Difficulty communicating in a relationship
- Valuing the approval of others more than valuing yourself
- Lacking trust in yourself & having poor self- esteem
- Having fears of abandonment or an obsessive need for approval
- Having an unhealthy dependence on relationships, even at your own cost

- Having a sense of responsibility for the actions of others

Abuse

- Partner accuses you of cheating
- Blames you for abuse
- Criticizes you
- Controls your money, friends, how you spend your time
- Yells at you and say's hurtful things
- Threatens you and or hits you
- Makes you feel like no one other than them loves you
- Embarrasses you in front of others & makes you want to

avoid people

Toxic

- You have to always be on defense
- He/She doesn't encourage your passions
- He/She doesn't accept your flaws
- He/She doesn't trust you
- He/She are always creating conflict with you
- You don't feel safe or comfortable and your always on edge

If you or anyone you know are experiencing domestic abuse contact the national Domestic violence hotline 1-800-799-SAFE (7233) www.thehotline.org

ABOUT THE AUTHOR

Aleisia Gordon is a licensed Cosmetologist who specialize in Aesthetics. She was born in Philadelphia and raised in South Philly. Aleisia graduated from South Philadelphia High School and later from Keystone Job Corps Center where she received her certification in Security & Business Office Technology. Aleisia worked in the security field and the beauty industry for over a decade. She is currently the Owner of Serene Candi Wax the first twenty four hour spa in Philadelphia specializing in her own manufactured hard wax. She is also an advocate for domestic violence awareness.

.

Made in the USA
Middletown, DE
26 November 2022